Jnanavatar Swami Sriyukteswar Giri

ज्ञानाबतार स्वामी श्रीयुक्तेश्वरेन प्रणीतम्

कैवल्यदर्शनम्

THE

HOLY SCIENCE

BY

Jnanavatar Swami Sriyukteswar Giri

Martino Publishing
Mansfield Centre, CT
2013

Martino Publishing
P.O. Box 373,
Mansfield Centre, CT 06250 USA

ISBN 978-1-61427-455-1

© *2013 Martino Publishing*

Cover design by T. Matarazzo

ज्ञानाबतार स्वामी श्रीयुक्तेश्वरेन प्रणीतम्

कैवल्यदर्शनम्

THE

HOLY SCIENCE

BY

Jnanavatar Swami Sriyukteswar Giri

Published by
YOGODA SAT-SANGA SOCIETY OF INDIA
(Shyama Charan Mission)
Founder-President, Paramhansa Yogananda
Headquarters, Yogoda Math
Dakshineswar, P.O. Ariadaha,
24 Parganas, Bengal, India
249 Dwapara (1949 A.D.)

FOREWORD

Prophets of all lands and ages have succeeded in their God-quest. Entering a state of true illumination, *nirbikalpa samadhi*, these saints have realized the Supreme Reality behind all names and forms. Their wisdom and 'spiritual counsel have become the scriptures of the world. These, although outwardly differing by reason of the variegated cloaks of words, are all expressions—some open and clear, others hidden or symbolic—of the same basic truth of Spirit.

My gurudeva, Jyanavatar Swami Sri Yukteswar (1855-1936), of Serampore, was eminently fitted to discern the underlying unity between the scriptures of Christianity and *Sanatan Dharma*. Placing the holy texts on the spotless table of his mind, he was able to dissect them with the scalpel of intuitive reasoning, and to separate interpolations and wrong interpretations of scholars from the truths as originally given by the prophets.

It is due to Jyanavatar Swami Sri Yukteswar's unerring spiritual insight that it now becomes possible, through this book, to establish a fundamental harmony between the difficult Biblical chapter, *Revelation*, and the *Sankhya* philosophy of India.

As my Gurudeva has explained in his Introduction, these pages were written by him in obedience to a request made by Babaji, the holy gurudeva of Lahiri Mahasaya, who in turn was the gurudeva of Sri Yukteswar. I have written about the Christlike lives of these three great masters in my book, *Autobiography of a Yogi* (London : Rider & Co.).

The Sanskrit aphorisms cited in *The Holy Science* will shed much light on the *Bhagbad Gita* as well as on other great scriptures of India.

Paramhansa Yogananda

249 Dwapara (1949 A.D.)

INTRODUCTION.

चतुर्नवत्युत्त रशतवर्षे गते द्वापरस्य प्रयागक्षेत्रे ।
सदर्शनविज्ञानमन्वयार्थं परंगुरुराजस्याज्ञान्तुप्राप्ता ॥
कड़ारवंश्य प्रियनाथस्वामी कादम्बिनीक्षेत्रनाथात्मजेन ।
हताय विश्वस्य बिदग्धतुष्णैः प्रणीतं दर्शनकैवल्यमेतत् ॥

The purpose of this book is to show as clearly as possible that there is an essential unity in all religions ; that there is no difference in the truths inculcated by the various faiths ; that there is but one method by which the world, both external and internal, has evolved; and that there is but one Goal admitted by all scriptures. But this basic truth is one not easily comprehended. The discord existing between the different religions, and the ignorance of men, make it almost impossible to lift the veil and have a look at this grand verity. The creeds foster a spirit of hostility and dissension ; ignorance widens the gulf that separates one creed from another. Only a few specially gifted persons can rise superior to the influence of their professed creeds and find absolute unanimity in the truths propagated by all great faiths.

The object of this book is to point out the harmony underlying the various religions, and to help in binding them together. This task is indeed a herculean one, but, at Allahabad, I was entrusted with the mission by a holy command. Allahabad, the sacred *Prayag-tirtha*, the place of confluence of the Ganges, Jumna, and Saraswati rivers, is a site for the congregation of worldly men and of spiritual devotees at the time of *Kumbha Mela*.

Worldly men cannot transcend the mundane limit in which they have confined themselves; nor can spiritual devotees, having once renounced the world, deign to come down and mix themselves in its turmoil. Yet men, who are wholly engrossed in earthly concerns, stand in infinite need of help and guidance from those holy beings who bring light to the race. So a place there must be where union between the two sets is possible. *Tirtha* affords such a meeting place. Situated as it is on the beach of the world, storms and buffets touch it not; the sadhus with a message for the benefit of humanity find a *Kumbha Mela* to be an ideal place to impart instruction to those who can heed it.

A message of such a nature I was chosen to propagate when I paid a visit to the *Kumbha Mela* being held at Allahabad in January, 1894. As I was walking along the bank of the Ganges, I was summoned by a man and was afterwards honoured by an interview with a great holy person, Babaji, the gurudeva of my own guru Lahiri Mahasaya of Benares. This holy personage at the *Kumbha Mela* was thus my own Param-Guruji-Maharaj, though this was our first meeting. During my conversation with Babaji, we spoke of the particular classes of men who now frequent these places of pilgrimage. I humbly suggested that there were men greater by far in intelligence than those then present, men who were living in distant parts of the world—Europe and America—professing different creeds, and ignorant of the real significance of the *Kumbha Mela*. They were men fit to hold communion with the spiritual devotees, so far as their intelligence is concerned, yet such intellectual men in foreign lands were alas ! wedded, in many cases, to rank materialism. Some of them, though famous for their investigations in the realms of science and philosophy, do not recognize the essential unity in religion. The professed creeds serve as nearly insurmountable barriers that threaten to separate mankind for ever.

My Param-Guruji-Maharaj, Babaji, smiled and, honouring me with the title of Swami, imposed on me the task of this book. I was chosen, I do not know the reason why, to remove the barrier and to help in establishing the basic truth in all religions.

The book is divided into four sections, according to the four stages in the development of knowledge. The highest aim of religion is *Atmajyanam*, Self-knowledge. But to attain this, knowledge of the external world is necessary. Therefore the first section of the book deals with वेद the gospel, and seeks to establish the fundamental truth of creation, and to describe the evolution and the involution of the world.

All creatures, from the highest to the lowest in the link of creation, are found eager to realize three things— Existence, Consciousness, and Bliss. This, the purpose or goal of all creatures, is the subject for discussion in the second section of the book. The third section deals with the method of realizing the three purposes of life. The fourth section discusses the revelations which come to those who have travelled far to realize the three ideals of life and are very near their destination.

The method I have adopted in the book is first to enunciate a proposition in Sanskrit terms of the Oriental sages, and then to explain it by reference to the holy scriptures of the West. In this way I have tried my best to show that there is no real discrepancy, much less any real conflict, between the teachings of the East and the West. Written as the book is under the inspiration of my Param-Guru-Deva, and in a Dwapara Age of rapid development in all departments of knowledge, I hope that the significance of the book will not be missed by those for whom it is meant.

A short discussion with mathematical calculation of the *Yugas* is necessary here in order to explain the fact that the present age for the world is Dwapara Yuga, and that 194 years of that *Yuga* have now (A.D. 1894) passed away, bringing a rapid development in man's knowledge.

We learn from Oriental astronomy that moons revolve around their planets, and planets turning on their axis revolve with their moons round the sun, and the sun again, with its planets and their moons, takes some star for its dual and revolves round it in about 24,000 years of our earth—a celestial phenomenon which causes the backward movement of the equinoctial points around the zodiac. The sun also has another motion by which it revolves round a grand centre called Bishnu-navi which is the seat of the creative power *Brahma*, the universal magnetism. *Brahma* regulates *Dharma* the mental virtues of the internal world. When the sun in its revolution round its dual comes to the place nearest to this grand centre the seat of *Brahma* (an event which takes place when the autumnal equinox comes to the first point of Aries) *Dharma* the mental virtue becomes so much developed that man can easily comprehend all, even the mysteries of Spirit.

DIAGRAM

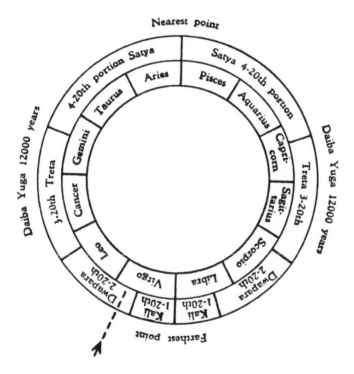

The Autumnal Equinox is now falling (at the beginning of the twentieth century) among the fixed stars of Virgo constellation, and in the early part of the Ascending Dwapara Yuga.

After 12,000 years, when the sun goes to the place in its orbit which is farthest from *Brahma* the grand centre (an event which takes place when the autumnal equinox is on the first point of Libra), *Dharma*, the mental virtue, comes to such a reduced state that man cannot grasp anything beyond the gross material creation.   Again, in the same manner, when the sun in its course of revolution begins to advance toward the place nearest to the grand centre, *Dharma*, the mental virtue, begins to develop ; this growth is gradually completed in another 12,000 years.

Each of these periods of 12,000 years brings about a complete change in the system, both externally in the material world, and internally in the intellectual or electric world, and is called one of the *Daiba Yugas* or Electric Couple.   Thus, in a period òf 24,000 years, the sun completes the revolution around its dual and finishes one electric cycle consisting of 12,000 years in an ascending arc, and 12,000 years in a descending arc.

Development of *Dharma*, the mental virtue, is but gradual and is divided into four different stages in a period of 12,000 years.   The time of 1200 years during which the sun passes through 1/20th portion of its orbit (*see* Diagram) is called Kali Yuga ; *Dharma*, the mental virtue, is then in its first stage and is only a quarter developed; the human intellect cannot comprehend anything beyond the gross material of this ever-changing creation, the external world.   The period of 2400 years during which the sun passes through the 2/20th portion of its orbit is called Dwapara Yuga; *Dharma*, the mental virtue, is then in the second stage of its development and is but half complete; the human intellect can then comprehend the fine matters or electricities and their attributes which are the creating principles of this external world.

The period of 3600 years during which the sun passes through the 3/20th part of its orbit is called Treta Yuga ; *Dharma*, the mental virtue, is then in the third stage ; the human intellect becomes able to comprehend the divine magnetism, the source of all electrical forces on which the creation depends for its existence. The period of 4800 years during which the sun passes through the remaining 4/20th portion of its orbit on either side of the point nearest the grand centre is called Satya Yuga ; *Dharma*, the mental virtue, is then in its fourth stage and completes its full development ; the human intellect can comprehend all, even God the Spirit beyond this visible world.

Manu, a great rishi of Satya Yuga., describes in his *Samhita* these *Yugas* more clearly in the following slokas :

"चत्वार्याहु: सहस्राणि वर्षनान्तु कृतं युगं ।
तस्य तावच्छतीसन्ध्या सन्ध्यांशश्च तथाविध: ॥
इतरेषु ससन्ध्यासु ससन्ध्यांशेषु च त्रिषु ।
एकापायेन वर्त्तन्ते सहस्राणि शतानि च ॥
यदेतत् परिसंख्यातमादावेब चतुर्युगं ।
एतद्द्वादशसाहस्रं देवानां युगमुच्यते ॥
दैविकानां युगानान्तु सहस्रं परिसंख्यया ।
ब्राह्ममकमहज्ञेयं तावती रात्रिरेब च ॥"

The period of Satya Yuga is 4000 years in duration ; 400 years before and after Satya Yuga proper are its *sandhis* or periods of mutation with the preceding and the succeeding yugas respectively; hence 4800 years in all is the proper age of Satya Yuga. In the calculation of the period of other *Yugas* and *Yuga-Sandhis*, it is laid down that numerical one should be deducted from the numbers of both thousands and hundreds which indicated the periods of the previous *Yugas* and *Sandhis*. From this rule it appears that 3000 years is the length of Treta Yuga, and 300 years before and after are its *Sandhis* the period of mutation, which make a total of 3600 years.

So 2000 years is the age of Dwapara Yuga, with 200 years before and after as its *sandhis* ; a total of 2400 years. Lastly, 1000 years is the length of Kali Yuga, with 100 years before and after as its *sandhis* ; a total of 1200 years. Thus 12,000 years, the sum total of all periods of these four yugas, is the length of one of the *Daiba Yugas* or Electric Couple, two of which, *i.e.*, 24,000 years, make the electric cycle complete. 100,000 of such *Daiba Yugas* is the Day of Brahma, the Creative Power or Creator, when creation exists in a manifested state ; the period equal to the above is its night when this creative power sleeps and the creation is dissolved.

From April 11, 501 B. C. when the autumnal equinox was on the first point of Aries, the sun began to move away from the point of its orbit nearest to the grand centre toward the point farthest from it, and accordingly the intellectual power of man began to diminish. During the 4800 years which the sun took to pass through one of the Satya couples or 4/20th part of its orbit, the intellect of man lost altogether the power of grasping the spiritual knowledge. During the 3600 years following, which the sun took to pass through the descending Treta Yuga, the intellect gradually lost all power of grasping the knowledge of divine magnetism. During the 2400 years next following, while the sun passed through descending Dwapara Yuga, the human intellect lost its power of grasping the knowledge of electricities and their attributes. In 1200 more years, during the year A. D. 499, the sun had passed through the descending Kali Yuga and had reached the point in its orbit which is farthest from the grand centre ; the autumnal equinox was on the first point of Libra. The intellectual power of man was so much diminished that it could no longer comprehend anything beyond the gross material of creation. The period around A. D. 500 was thus the darkest part of Kali Yuga and of the whole cycle of 24,000 years. History indeed bears out the accuracy of these ancient calculations of the Indian rishis, and records the widespread ignorance and suffering in all nations at that period.

From A. D. 499 onwards, the sun began to advance toward the grand centre, and the intellect of man started gradually to develop. During 1100 years of the Ascending Kali Yuga, which brings us to A. D. 1599, the human intellect was so dense that it could not comprehend the electricities, *Sukshmabhuta*, the fine matters of creation. In the political world, also, generally speaking there was no peace in any kingdom.

Subsequent to this period, when the 100-year transitional *sandhi* of Kali Yuga set in, to effect a union with the following Dwapara Yuga, men began to notice the existence of fine matters, the attributes of five electricities, *Panchatunmatra* ; and political peace began to be established.

About A. D. 1600, William Gilbert discovered magnetic forces, and observed the presence of electricity in all material substances. In 1609 Kepler discovered important laws of astronomy, and Galileo produced a telescope. In 1621 Drebbel of Holland invented the microscope. About 1670 Newton discovered the law of gravitation. Thomas Savery made use of a steam engine in raising water about 1700. Twenty years later Stephen Gray discovered the action of electricity on the human body.

In the political world, people began to have respect for themselves, and civilization advanced in many ways. England united with Scotland became a powerful kingdom. Nepoleon Bonaparte introduced his new legal code into southern Europe. America won its independence, and Europe was peaceful in many parts. With the advance of science, the world began to be covered with railways and telegraphic wires. By the help of steam engines, electric machines, and many other instruments, fine matters were brought into practical use, although their nature was not clearly understood.

After 1899, on the completion of the period of 200 years
of *Dwapara Sandhi*, the time of mutation, the true
Dwapara Yuga of 2000 years will commence and will
give to mankind in general a thorough understanding
of the electrical attributes.

Such is the great influence of Time which governs
the universe. No man can overcome this influence
except he who, blessed with pure love, the heavenly
gift of nature, becomes divine ; being baptised in the
sacred stream *Pranava* (the holy *Aum* vibration), he
comprehends the kingdom of God.

The position of the world in the *Dwapara Sandhi* era
at present (A. D. 1894) is not correctly shown in the
Hindu almanacs. The astronomers and astrologers who
calculate the almanacs have been guided by wrong
annotations of certain Sanskrit scholars (such as Kullu
Bhatta) of the dark age of Kali Yuga, and now maintain
that the length of Kali Yuga is 432,000 years, of which
4994 have (in A. D. 1894) passed away, leaving 427,006
years still remaining. A dark prospect ! and fortunately
one not true. The mistake crept into the almanac for
the first time about 700 B. C., during the time of Raja
Parikshita, just after the completion of the last Descending Dwapara Yuga. At that time Maharaja Judhisthir,
noticing the appearance of the dark Kali Yuga, made
over his throne to his grandson the said Raja Parikshita.
Maharaja Judhisthir, together with all the wise men
of his court, retired to the Himalaya Mountains, the
paradise of the world. Thus there was none in the

court af Raja Parikshita who could understand the
principle of correctly calculating the ages ?of the several
yugas. Hence, after the completion of the 2400 years
of the then-current Dwapara Yuga, no one dared to
make the introduction of the dark Kali Yuga more
manifest by beginning to calculate from its first year
and to put an end to the number of Dwapara years.
According to this wrong method of calculation, therefore, the first year of Kali Yuga was numbered 2401
along with the age of Dwapara Yuga. In A. D. 499,
when 1200 years, the length of the true Kali Yuga was
complete, and the sun had reached the point of its orbit
farthest from the grand centre (when the autumnal
equinox was on the first point of Libra in the heavens),
the age of Kali in its darkest period was then numbered
by 3600 years instead of by 1200.

With the commencement of the Ascending Kali Yuga,
after A. D. 499, the sun began to advance in its orbit
nearer to the grand centre, and accordingly the intellectual power of man started to develop. Therefore
the mistake in the almanacs began to be noticed by
the wise men of the time, who found that the calculations of the ancient rishis had fixed the period of
one Kali Yuga at 1200 years only. But as the intellect of these wise men was not yet suitably developed,
they could make out only the mistake itself, and not
the reason for it. By way of reconciliation, they
fancied that 1200 years, the real age of Kali, were
not the ordinary years of our earth, but were so many
Daiba years consisting of 12 *Daiba* months of 30 *Daiba*

days each, with each *Daiba* day being equal to one ordinary solar year of our earth. Hence according to these men 1200 years of Kali Yuga must be equal to 432,000 years of our earth.

In coming to a right conclusion, however, we should take into · consideration the position of the vernal equinox at spring in the year 1893.

The astronomical reference books show the equinox now to be 20° 54′ 36″ distant from the first point of Aries (the fixed star Revati), and by calculation it will appear that 1394 years have passed away since the time when the vernal equinox began to recede from the first point of Aries.

Deducting 1200 years (the length of the last Ascending Kali Yuga) from 1394 years, we get 194 to indicate the present year of the world's entrance into the Ascending Dwapara Yuga. The mistake of older almanacs will thus be clearly explained when we add 3600 years to this period of 1394 years, and get 4994 years—which according to the prevailing mistaken theory now represents the present year (A. D. 1894) in the Hindu almanacs.

(Referring to the Diagram given in this book, the reader will see that the Autumnal Equinox is now (A. D. 1894) falling among the stars of the Virgo constellation, and in the Ascending Dwapara Yuga.)

In this book certain truths such as those about the properties of magnetism, its auras, different sorts of electricities, etc., have been mentioned although modern science has not yet fully discovered them. As for the five sorts of electricity, it may be observed here that they can be easily understood if one will direct his attention to the nerve properties which are purely electrical in nature. Each of the five sensory nerves has its characteristic and unique function to perform. The optic nerve carries light and does not perform the functions of the auditory and other nerves; the auditory nerve in its turn carries sound only without performing the functions of any other nerves, and so on. Thus it is clear that there are five sorts of electricity, corresponding to the five properties of cosmic electricity.

So far as magnetic properties are concerned, it may be remembered that the grasping power of the human intellect is at present so limited that it would be quite useless to attempt to make the matter understood by the general public. The intellect of men in Treta Yuga will comprehend the attributes of divine magnetism (the next Treta Yuga will start in A. D. 4099). There are indeed exceptional personages now living who, having overcome the influence of time, can grasp today what ordinary people cannot grasp; but this book is not for those exalted ones, who require nothing of it.

In concluding this introduction, we may observe that the different planets, exercising their influence over the various days of the week, have lent their names to their respective days; similarly, the different constellations of stars, having influence over various months, have lent their names to the Hindu months. Each of the great Yugas also has much influence over the period of time covered by it ; hence, in designating the years it is desirable that such terms should indicate to which Yuga they belong.

As the Yugas are calculated from the position of the equinox, the method of numbering the years in reference to their respective Yuga is based on a scientific principle; its use will obviate much inconvenience which has arisen in the past owing to the various eras being associated with persons of eminence rather than with celestial phenomena of the fixed stars. We, therefore, propose to name and number the year in which this introduction has been written as 194 Dwapara, instead of A. D. 1894, to show the exact time of the Yuga now passing. This method of calculation was prevalent in India till the reign of Raja Vikramaditya, when the *Sambat* era was introduced. As the Yuga method of calculation recommends itself to reason, we follow it, and recommend that it be followed by the public in general.

Now, in this 194th year of Dwapara Yuga, the dark age of Kali having long passed away, the world is reaching out for spiritual knowledge, and men require loving help one from the other. The publishing of this book, requested from me by my holy Param-Guru Maharaj, will, I hope, be of spiritual service.

SWAMI SRIYUKTESWAR GIRI

Serampore, Bengal.
The 26th Falgun, 194 Dwapara.
(A. D. 1894)

2

कैवल्यदर्शनम्

CHAPTER I

वेदः THE GOSPEL

नित्यं पूर्णमनाह्यनन्तंवृह्मपरमं
तदेवेकमेवाढैतं सत् ॥ १ ॥

The Eternal Father God *Swami Parambrahma* is the only Real Substance, *Sat*, and is all in all in the universe.

Man possesses eternal faith and believes intuitively

Why God is not comprehensible.

in the existence of a substance, of which the objects of sense—sound, touch, sight, taste, and smell, the component parts of this visible world—are but properties. As man identifies himself with his material body composed of the aforesaid properties he is able to comprehend by his imperfect organs these properties only and not the substance to which these properties belong. The Eternal Father God, the only substance in the universe is, therefore, not comprehensible by man of this material world, unless he becomes divine by lifting his self above this creation of Darkness *Maya* Vide Hebrew XI. 1. and John VIII. 28.

"Now faith is the substance of things hoped for, the evidence of things not seen."

*"Then said Jesus unto them, When ye have lifted
up the Son of man, then shall ye know that I am He———."*

तत् सब्बेंज्ञप्रेमबीजश्चित्

सब्बेशक्ति बीजमानन्दश्च ॥ १ ॥

2. The Almighty Force *Shakti* or in other words,
'Prakriti' the the Eternal Joy *Ananda* which produces
Nature. the world, and the Omniscient Feeling
Chit which makes this world conscious, demonstrate
the Nature *Prakriti* of God the Father.

As man is the likeness of God, directing his atten-
How compre- tion inwards he can comprehend within
hended. him the said Force and Feeling, the sole
properties of his self :—the Force Almighty as his will
Basana with enjoyment *Bhoga*, and the Feeling Omniscient as his Consciousness *Chetana* that enjoys *Bhokta.*
Vide Genesis I. 27.

*"So God created man in his own image, in the image
of God created he him ; male and female created he
them."*

तच्छब्बेशक्तिदीजजड़प्रकृतिबासनाया: व्यक्तभाव:

प्रएबशब्द: दिक्कालानबोऽपि तस्य रूपा: ॥ ३ ॥

3. The manifestation of Omnipotent Force (Repul-
sion, in its complementary portion Omniscient Feeling
The word, or Love the Attraction) is vibration which
"Amen," appears as a peculiar sound, the Word
"Aum," is the
beginning of Amen *Aum.* In its different aspects Aum
the Creation. presents the idea of change, which is
Time *Kal*, in the Ever-unchangeable ; and the idea

of division, which is Space *Desh*, in the Ever-indivisible.

The Four Aspects. The word, time, space, and atom.
The ensuing effect is the idea of particles —the innumerable atoms *patra* or *anu*. These four, viz., the Word, Time, Space and Atom, therefore, are one and the same, and substantially nothing but mere ideas.

This manifestation the Word, becoming Flesh the external material, created this visible world. So this Word Amen *Aum*, being the manifestation of the Eternal Nature of the Almighty Father or His Own Self, is inseparable from and nothing but God Him-self ; as the Burning Power is inseparable from and nothing but the Fire itself. Vide Rev. III. 14 and John I. 1, 3, 14.

"*These things saith the Amen, the faithful and true witness, the beginning of the Creation of God*"

"*In the beginning was the Word, and the Word was with God, and the word was God—all things were made by Him ; and without Him was not anything made that was made—and the Word was made flesh and dwelt among us.*"

नदेब जगत्कारएमाया ईश्वरस्य,

तस्य व्यष्टिरविद्या ॥ ४ ॥

4. These Atoms, which represent within and with-out the four ideas mentioned above, are the Thrones

Atoms the throne of the Creator.
of Spirit the Creator that shining on them creates this universe. They are called en-masse *Maya* the Darkness, as

they keep the Spiritual Light out of comprehension ;
and each of them separately is called *Abidya* the
Ignorance, as it makes man ignorant even of his own
self. Hence the aforesaid four ideas which give rise
to all those cofusions are mentioned in the Bible as
so many beasts. Man, so long as he identifies himself with his gross material body, holds a position
far inferior to that of the Primal four fold Atoms and
necessarily fails to coprehend the same. But when
he raises himself to the level thereof he not only
comprehends 'this Atom both inside and outside, but
also the whole creation, both unmanifested and manifested (i. e., "before and behind"). Vide Rev. IV. 6.

"And in the midst of the throne, and round about
the throne, were four beasts full of eyes before and
behind."

तच्छब्बंज्ञप्रेमबीजं परा, तदेव कूटस्थचैतन्य:

पुरूषोत्तम:, तस्याभास: पुरूष: तस्मादभेद: ॥ ५ ॥

5. The manifestation of *Prembijam Chit* Attraction the Omniscient Love, is Life the Omnipresent
Holy Spirit and is called the Holy Ghost

Kutastha-
Chaitanya the
Holy Ghost
Purushottama

Kutastha Chaitanya or *Purushottama* which
shines on Darkness *Maya* to attract
every portion of it towards Divinity.
But the Darkness *Maya* or its individual parts *Abidya*
the Ignorance being repulsion itself cannot receive or
comprehend the Spiritual Light but reflects it. This
Holy Ghost being the manifestation of the Omniscient

Nature of the Eternal Father God is no other subs-
Avas-Chai-
tanya or
Purush the
sons of God tance than God Himself ; and so these reflections of Spiritual rays are called the Sons of God *Avaschaitanya* or *Purush.*
Vide John I. 4, 5, 11.

"*In Him was Life ; and the Life was the Light of men.*"

"*And the Light shineth in Darkness ; and the Darkness comprehended it not.*"

"*He came unto his own, and his own received him not.*"

चिच्छकाशादनोर्मंहृत्वंतन्चित्वम्, तत् सदध्यवसाय

सत्व: बुद्धि:, ततस्तद्विपरीतं मन: च रमेऽभिमानोऽ-

हंकारस्थदेव जीव: ॥ ६ ॥

6. This Atom *Abidya* the Ignorance being under the influence of Universal Love *Chit* the Holy Spirit becomes spiritualised like iron filings in magnetic
Chittwa the
Heart. aura, and possessed of consciousness the power of feeling, when it is called *Mahot* the Heart *Chittwa*, and being such the idea of separate
Ego, Ahamkar,
the Son of
Man. existence of self appears in it, which is called *Ahamkar* Ego the son of Man. Thus being magnetized it gets two poles ; one of which attracts it towards the Real Substance
Buddhi, the
Intelligence. *Sat,* and the other repels it from the same. The former is called *Sattwa* or *Buddhi* the Intelligence which determines what is truth ; and the latter, which being a particle of Repulsion, the Almighty Force spiritualised as aforesaid, produces

(6)

the ideal world for enjoyment *ananda*, and is called
Anandatwa or *Manas* the Mind.

Manas, the Mind

तदहंकाराचित्तबिकारपञ्चतन्त्रानि ॥ ७ ॥

तान्येब कारणशरीर: पुरूषस्य ॥ ८ ॥

तेषां तिगुणेभ्य: पञ्चदशबिषयेन्द्रियानि ॥ ९ ॥

एतानि मनोबुद्धिभ्यां सह सप्तदशसूक्ष्माङ्गानि
लिङ्गशरीरस्व ॥ १० ॥

7-10 This spritualised Atom *Chittwa* the Heart being
the Repulsion manifested produces five sorts of aura—
electricities—from its five different parts : one from the
middle, two from the two extremities, and the other two
from the spaces intervening between the middle and each
of the extremities. These five sorts of electricities being
attracted under the influence of Uni-
versal Love the Holy Ghost towards the
Real Substance *Sat* produce a magnetic
field which is called the body of *Sattwa
Buddhi* the Intelligence. These five electricities being
the causes of all other creations are called *Pancha-
Tattwa* the five Root-causes and are named as Causal
body of *Purush* the Son of God.

Pancha-Tattwa the Root Causes of creation is the Causal body.

These Electricities being evolved from the polarised
Chittwa are also in a polarised state
and are endowed with its three attributes or *Gunas*—*Sattwa* the positive,
Tama the negative, and *Rajas* the neutralising.

Three Gunas the electric attributes

The positive attributes of these five electricities are **Jnyanendriyas** the organs of sense—organs of smell, taste, sight, touch, and hearing—and being attracted under the influence of *manas* Mind the opposite pole of this Spiritualised Atom constitutes a body of the same. The neutralising attributes of them are *Karmendriyas* the organs of action—those of excretion, generation, motion, absorption, and articulation. These organs being the manifestation of the neutralising energy of the Spiritualised Atom *Chittwa* the Heart constitutes an energetic body called the body of energy the life *Pran*. And their negative attributes are the five Tanmatras or objects of the senses of smell, taste, sight, touch, and sound which, through the neutralising power of the organs of action being united with the organs of sense, satiate the desires of the Heart.

Jnyanendriyas the five organs of sense

Karmendriyas the five organs of action.

Bishaya or Tanmatras the five objects of Senses

These fifteen attributes with two poles—Mind and Intelligence—of the spiritualised Atom constitute *Lingasharir* or *Sukshma-sharir* the fine material body of *Purush* the son of God.

Linga-Sharir, the fine material body.

ततपञ्चतत्वानां स्थितिशौलतामसिक बिषयपञ्चतन्मात्रानां

पञ्चिकरणेन स्युलशरीरस्याङ्गानि जड़ीभूतपञ्चक्षिल्यप्तेज-

मरुह्योमान्युद्भुतानि ॥ ११ ॥

एतान्येब चतुर्बिंशतितत्वानि: ॥ १२ ॥

11-12. The aforesaid five objects, which are the negative attributes of the five electricities, being combined together produce the idea of the gross matters which appear to us in five different varieties, viz., *Kshiti* the Solid, *Ap* the Liquid, *Tej* the fiery, *Marut* the gaseous, and *Byoma* or *Akasha* the Ethereal ; these
Gross material body. constitute the outer covering called *Sthulsharir* the gross material body of *Purush* the son of God.

These five gross matters and the aforesaid fifteen attributes together with *Manas* the Mind, *Buddhi* the Intelligence, *Chittwa* the Heart, and
Twenty four Elders. *Ahamkar* the Ego, constitute the twenty-four principles or Elders as mentioned in the Bible. Vide Rev. IV. 4.

"*And round about the throne were four and twenty seats ; and upon the seats I saw four and twenty Elders.*"

The aforesaid twenty-four principles which completed the creation of Darkness *Maya* are nothing but mere development of Ignorance *Abidya* ; and this Ignorance being composed only of ideas as mentioned above, this creation has no substantial existence in reality but is a mere play of ideas on the Eternal Substance God the Father.

तत्त्ँब चतुर्द्दशभुबनानिब्यास्ख्यातानि ॥ १३ ॥

13. This universe thus described commencing from
Seven Spheres the Eternal Substance God down to the
or Swargas. gross material creation has been distingui-
shed into seven different spheres, *Swargas or Lokas.*

(a) The foremost of these is *Satyaloka* the sphere of
7th Sphere God the only Real Substance *Sat* in the
Satayaloka. universe. No name can describe it, nor
can anything in the creation of Darkness or Light
designate it.

This sphere is therefore called *Anam* the Nameless.

(b) The next in order is *Tapaloka* the sphere of the
6th Sphere Holy Spirit which is the Eternal Patience
Tapaloka. as it remains for ever undisturbed by any
limited idea ; and because it is not approachable even by
the Sons of God as such it is called. *Agam* the Inacces-
sible.

(c) Next is *Janaloka* the sphere of spiritual reflection,
5th sphere the sons of God, wherein the idea of
Janaloka. separate existence of Self originates. As
this sphere is above the comprehension of anybody in
the creation of Darkness *Maya,* it is called *Alakshya* the
Incomprehensible.

(d) Then comes *Maharloka,* the sphere of Atom, the
4th Sphere beginning of the creation of Darkness
Maharloka. *Maya* upon which the Spirit is reflected.
This, the connecting link, is the only way between the
spiritual and material creation and is called the Door
Dasamadwar.

(e) Around this Atom is *Sivaloka* the sphere of
3rd Sphere Sivaloka. magnetic aura, the electricities. This
sphere, being characterised by the absence
of all the creation, even the organs and their objects the
fine material things, is called *Mahashunya* the great
Vacuum.

(f) The next is *Bhubaloka* the electric attributes. As
2nd Sphere Bhubaloka. the gross matters of the creation are
entirely absent from this sphere, and it is
conspicuous by the presence of the fine matters only, it
is called *Shunya* the vacuum ordinary.

(g) The last and lowest sphere is *Bhuloka* the sphere
1st Sphere Bhuloka. of gross material creation, which is always
visible to everybody.

As God created man in his own image, so is the body
Sapta Patals or seven churches. of man like unto the image of this universe. The material body of man has
also seven vital places within it called
Patals. Man, turning towards his self and advancing in
the right way, perceives the Spiritual Light in these
places which are described in the Bible as so many
Churches ; the Lights like stars perceived therein are as
so many Angels. Vide Rev. I. 12, 13, 16, 20.

"*And being turned, I saw seven golden candlesticks.—And
in the midst of the seven candlesticks one like unto the Son
of man.*"

"*And he had in his right hand seven stars.*"

"*The seven stars are the angels of the seven churches ; and the seven candlesticks which thou sawest are the seven churches.*"

The above-mentioned Seven Spheres or *Swargas* and seven Patals constitute the Fourteen Bhubans the fourteen distinguishable stages of the creation.

Fourteen Bhubans the stages of creation.

तान्येब पङ्कुकोषानि पुरूषस्य ॥ १४ ॥

14. This *Purush* the Son of God is screened by five coverings called *Koshas* Sheaths.

Five Koshas or Sheaths.

I. The first of these five is Heart *Chittwa* the Atom composed of four ideas, as mentioned before, which feels or enjoys and thus being the seat of enjoyment *ananda* is called *Anandamoya Kosha.*

Heart the1st. Kosha.

II. The second is the magnetic aura electricities, manifestations of Buddhi the intelligence which determines what is truth. Thus being the seat of knowledge *jnyan*, it is called *Jnyanamoya Kosha.*

Buddhi the 2nd Kosha.

III. The third is the body of *Manas* the Mind, composed of the organs of sense as mentioned above, and is called the *Manamaya Kosha.*

"Manas" the 3rd Kosha.

IV. The fourth is the body of energy, life force or
"Pran" the   *Pran*, composed of the organs of action
4th Kosha.   as described before, and so is called the
Pranamaya kosha.

V. The fifth and the last of these sheaths is the
Gross-matters   gross matter, the Atom's outer coating,
the 5th Kosha.   which becoming *Anna* the nourishment
supports this visible world, and thus is called the
Annamoya Kosha.

The action of Repulsion the manifestation of the
Action of   Omnipotent Energy being thus completed,
Love.   the action of Attraction (the manifestation of the Omniscient Love in the core of the heart)
begins to be manifested. Under the influence of this
Omniscient Love the attraction, the Atoms being attracted towards one another come nearer and nearer, taking
Innanimate   Ethereal, Gaseous, Fiery, Liquid, and
Kingdom,   Solid forms. Thus this visible world
becomes adorned with suns, planets, and moons which
we call the inanimate kingdom of the creation.

In this manner when the action of the Divine Love
Vegetable   becomes well developed, the evolution of
Kingdom.   *Avidya* Ignorance (the particle of Darkness
Maya the Omnipotent Energy manifested) begins to be
withdrawn. *Annamoya Kosha* the Atom's outer coating
of gross matter being thus with-drawn, *Pranamaya
Kosha* (the sheath composed of *Karmendriya* the organs
of action) begin to operate. In this organic state the

Atoms embracing each other more close to their heart
appears to us as the vegetable kingdom in the creation.

When the *Pranamaya Kosha* becomes withdrawn, the
Animal   *Manamaya Kosha* (the sheath composed
Kingdom   of *jnyanendriyas* the organs of sense)
comes to the light. The Atoms then perceive the nature
of the external world and, attracting other atoms of
different nature, form bodies as necessary for enjoyment,
and thus the animal Kingdom appears in the creation.

When *Manamaya Kosha* becomes withdrawn, *Jnyana-
Mankind   maya Kosha* (the body of Intelligence
composed of electricities) becomes per-
ceptible. The Atom, getting the power of determining
right and wrong, becomes man the rational being in the
creation.

When man cultivating the Divine Spirit, Omniscient
Devata or   Love, within his heart can withdraw this
Angel.   *Jnyanamaya Kosha*, then the innermost
sheath *Chittwa* the Heart (composed of four ideas) becomes manifested. Man is then called *Debata* or Angel
in the creation.

When the Heart or innermost sheath is also with
Free Sannyasi   drawn, there is no longer anything
to keep man in bondage to this crea-
tion of Darkness *Maya*. He then becomes free, *Sannyasi*
the son of God, and enters into the creation of
Light.

(14)

स्थुलज्ञानक्रमात् सूक्ष्मबिषयेन्द्रि यज्ञानं स्वप्नवत् ॥ १५ ॥

तत्क्रमात् मनोबुद्धिज्ञानञ्चायतथिति परीक्ष: ॥ १६ ॥

15-16. When man compares his ideas relating to
Sleeping and gross matters conceived in the wakeful
waking states state, with his conception of ideas in
dream, the similarity existing between them naturally
leads him to conclude this external world also is not
what it appears to be. When he looks for further
explanation he finds that all his wakeful conceptions
are substantially nothing but mere ideas caused by
the union of five objects of sense—the negative attributes of the five internal electricities—with the five
organs of sense their positive attributes—through the
medium of five organs of action—the neutralizing
attributes of the electricities. This union is effected
by the operation of Mind *Manas* and conceived by the
Intelligence *Buddhi*. Thus it is clear that all conceptions which man forms in his wakeful state are mere
inferential *Parokshajnyan*—a matter of inference only.

तत: सद्गुरूलाभ: भक्तियोगश्च तेना।परोक्ष: ॥ १७ ॥

17. In this way, when man understands by his
When man *Parokshajnyan* the nothingness of the ex-
gets Sat Guru ternal world, he appreciates the position
the Preceptor. of John, the Divine personage who wit-
nessed Light and bore testimony of Christ after his
heart's love, the heavenly gift of Nature, had become

developed. Any advanced sincere seeker may be fortunate in having the Godlike company of some one of
such personages who may kindly stand to him as his
Spiritual Preceptor, *Sat Guru*, the Saviour. Following
affectionately the holy precepts of these divine personages, man becomes able to direct all his organs inward
to their common centre—Sensorium, *Trikuti* or *Sushumnadwar*, the door of the interior—where he comprehends
Radha or John.   the voice, like a peculiar knocking sound
the Word Amen, *Aum*, and the God-
sent luminous body of *Radha*, called John in the
Bible. Vide Rev. III, 13, 20. John I. 6,8,23.

"*These things saith the Amen, the faithful and true
witness, the beginning of the creation of God.*"

"*Behold, I stand at the door, and knock ; if any man
hear my voice and open the door, I will come into
him and will sup with him, and he with me.*"

"*There was a man sent from God, whose name was
John.*"

"*He was not that Light, but was sent to bear witness of that Light.*"

"*He said, I am the voice of one crying in the wilderness, Make Straight the way of the Lord, as said the
prophet Esaias.*"

3

(16)

From the peculiar nature of this sound, issuing as

Ganga, Jumna or Jordan the holy Stream. it does like a stream from a higher unknown region and losing itself in the gross material creation, it is figuratively styled by various sects of people by the names of different rivers which they consider as sacred ; e. g., *Ganga* by the Aryans, *Jumna* by the *Baishnava*, Jordon by the Christians, etc.

Through his luminous body, man, believing in the

The 2nd birth existence of the true Light—the Life of this universe—becomes baptised or absorbed in the holy stream of the sound. This baptism is, so to speak, the second birth of man and is called *Bhakti yoga*, without which man can never become able to comprehend the real position of the internal world, the kingdom of God. Vide, John I. 9, and III. 3.

"*That was the true Light, which lighteth every man that cometh into the world.*"

"*Verily, verily I say unto thee, Except a man be born again, he cannot see the kingdom of God.*"

In this state the Son of man begins to repent (Lat.

Aparoksha Jnyan the real comprehension. *repens*, to creep) and turning back from the gross material creation creeps toward his Divinity, the Eternal Substance, God. When the development of Ignorance begins to recede, man gradually comprehends the true character of this creation of Darkness, *Maya*, as a mere ideal play of the Supreme Nature on his own self, the only Real Substance. This true comprehension is called *Aparokshajnyan.*

यदात्मानं परमात्मनि दर्शनन्ततः कैवल्यम् ॥ १८ ॥

18. When all the developments of Ignorance are
Sannyasi or Christ the anointed Saviour.
withdrawn, the Heart being perfectly clear and purified no longer merely reflects the Spiritual Light but receives or manifests the same, and thus being consecrated and anointed becomes *Sannyasi* or Christ the Saviour. Vide John I. 33.

'*Upon whom thou shalt see the Spirit descending, and remaining on him, the same is he which baptiseth with the Holy Ghost.*"

Through this Saviour, the Son of man becomes again
Christ or Sannyasi the Son of God.
baptised or absorbed in the stream of Spiritual Light and coming above the creation of Darkness *Maya*, enters into the spiritual world and becomes unified with *Abhas Chaitanya* or *Purush*, the Son of God, as was the case with Lord Jesus of Nazareth. This is the state when man is saved for ever and ever from the bondage of Darkness *Maya*. Vide John I. 12 and III. 5.

"*But as many as received him, to them gave he power to become the sons of God, even to them that believe on his name.*"

"*Verily, verily, I say unto thee, Except a man be born of water and of the Spirit, he cannot enter into the kingdom of God.*"

When man, thus entering into the spiritual world,
Sacrifice of self. becomes a Son of God, he comprehends the universal Light—the Holy Ghost—as a perfect whole, and his self as nothing but a mere idea resting on a fragment of the *Aum* Light. Then he sacrifices himself to the Holy Ghost the altar of God, i. e., abandons the vain idea of his separate existence and becomes one integral whole. Thus being one with the universal Holy Spirit of God the Father,
Kaivalya the unification. he becomes unified with the Real Substance, God. This unification of self with the Eternal substance God, is called *Kaivalya*, Vide Rev. III. 21.

"*To him that overcometh will I grant to sit with me in my throne, even as I also overcame, and am set down with my Father in his throne.*"

———

CHAPTER II

अभीष्ट: । THE GOAL

अत: मुक्तिजिज्ञासा ॥ १ ॥

1. When man understands even by way of inference
Liberation the   the true nature of this creation, the true
prime object.   relation existing between that creation
and himself, when he further understands that he is
completely blinded by the influence of Darkness, *Maya,*
and that it is the bondage of Darkness alone which
makes him forget his real self and brings about all his
sufferings, he naturally wishes to be relieved from all
these evils. This relief from evil, or the liberation from
the bondage of Darkness, *Maya,* becomes the prime
object of his life.

मुक्तिस्वरूपेऽबस्थानम् ॥ २ ॥

2. When man raises himself above the ideal creation
     of this Darkness, *Maya,* and passes
Residing in
self   completely out of its influence, he be-
Liberation.   comes liberated from bondage and is
placed in his real self the Eternal Spirit.

तदा सब्बंक्लेशनिबृत्ति: परमार्थसिद्धिश्च ॥ ३ ॥

3. On attaining this liberation, man becomes saved
Liberation is from all his troubles, and all the desires
Salvation. of his heart are fulfilled, so the ultimate
aim of his life is accomplished.

इतरत्र कामापूर्णो जन्मजन्मान्तरब्यापी

क्लेशमयदु:खम् ॥ ४ ॥

4. So long, however, as man identifies himself
Why man with his material body and fails to find
suffers. repose in his true self, he feels his wants
according as his hearts desires remain unsatisfied.
To satisfy them he has to appear often in flesh and
blood on the stage of life, subject to the influence
of Darkness, *Maya*, and has to suffer all the troubles
of life and death not only in the present but in the
future as well.

क्लेशमबिद्यामातृम् ॥ ५ ॥

भावेऽभावोऽभावेभाव इत्येवंरूपमबिद्या ॥ ६ ॥

5-6. Ignorance, *Abidya*, is misconception, or is the
What is erroneous conception of the existence of
Ignorance? that which does not exist. Through

abidya man believes that this material creation is the only thing which substantially exists, there being nothing beyond; forgetting that this material creation is substantially nothing and is a mere play of ideas on the Eternal Spirit, the only Real Substance beyond the comprehension of the material creation. This ignorance is not only a trouble in itself but is also the source of all other troubles of man.

तदेबाब रएविंज्ञेपशक्तिविशिष्टत्वात् क्षेतृमस्मिताभिनिबेश-

रागद्वेषानाम् ॥ ७ ॥

तस्याबरएशक्तैरस्मितैभिनिबेशी

बिक्षेपशक्तेश्च रागद्वेषौ ॥ ८ ॥

स्वामिशक्तोरबिबिक्त ज्ञानमम्मिता ॥ ९ ॥

प्राकृतिकसंस्कारमातृमभिनिबेश: ॥ १० ॥

सुखकरबिषयतृष्णा राग: ॥ ११ ॥

दु:खकरविषयत्यागतृष्णाद्वेष: ॥ १२ ॥

7-12. In order to understand how this Ignorance is

Ignorance is the Source of all troubles.

the source of all other troubles we should remember (as has been explained in the previous chapter) that Ignorance, *Abidya*, is nothing but a particle of Darkness, *Maya*, taken distributively, and as such it possesses the two properties of *maya*. The one is its darkening power by the influence of which man is prevented from grasping anything beyond the material creation. This darkening power produces *Asmita* or *Egoism* being the identification

of self with the material body which is but the development of Atom, the particles of the universal force ; and
Avinibesha or Tenacity to the Condition.   By virtue of
the second of the properties of *Maya*, Ignorance or *abidya*
in its polarised state produces an attraction for certain
objects and repulsion for others.   The objects so attracted are the objects of pleasure for which an Attachment,
Raga, is formed.   The objects that are repulsed are the
objects producing pain for which an Aversion, *Dwesha*,
is formed.

क्लेशमूल कर्म्मंत द्विपाक एव दुःखः ॥ १३ ॥

13. By the influence of these five troubles, viz.,
Why man   Ignorance, Egotism, Attachment, Aver-
works.   sion, and Tenacity to the material creation, man is induced to involve himself in egoistic works
and in consequence he suffers.

सर्व्वं दुःखानां निवृतिरित्यार्थं ॥ १४ ॥
निवृत्येपनुवृत्यभाबः परमः ॥ १५ ॥

14-15. With man the cessation of all sufferings is
Ultimate aim   *Artha*, the heart's immediate aim.   The
of the heart.   complete extirpation of all these suffer-

ings, their recurrence becoming impossible, is the *Paramartha*, the ultimate goal.

सर्ब्बंकामपूर्णत्वे सर्ब्बदुःखमूलक्लेशनिवृतिः
तदा परमार्थं सिद्धिः ॥ १६ ॥

सच्चिदानन्दमयत्वप्राप्तिरिति त्तियकामाः ॥ १७ ॥

सद्गुरूदत्तसाघनप्रभावात् चित्तस्य प्रसादः
एवानन्दः ॥ १८ ॥

ततः सर्ब्बदुःखानां हानन्तदा
सर्ब्बभाबोदयश्चित ॥ १९ ॥

ततः आत्मनो नित्यत्वोपलब्धिः सत् ॥ २० ॥

तदेव स्वरूपः पु पस्य ॥ २१ ॥

16-21. Man naturally feels great necessity for *Sat* Existence, *Chit* Consciousness, and *Ananda* Bliss. These three are the real necessities of the human heart and have nothing to do with anything outside his self. They are essential properties of his own nature, as explained in the previous chapter.

The real necessities.

When man becomes fortunate in securing the favour of any divine personage *Satguru* the Saviour, and affectionately following his holy precepts is able to direct all his organs inward, he becomes capable of satisfying all the wants of his heart and can thereby get contentment, *Ananda*, the Real Bliss.

How man gets Bliss

With his heart thus contented, man becomes able to
fix his attention upon anything he chooses
and can comprehend all its aspects. So
Chit Consciousness of all the modifica-
tions of Nature up to its first and primal manifestation
the Word Amen *Aum*, and even of his own Real Self,
gradually appears. And being absorbed in the stream
thereof, man becomes baptised and begins to repent
towards his Divinity the Eternal Father, whence he had
fallen. *Vide* Revelation II, 51.

How Cons-
ciousness
appears.

"*Remember therefore from whence thou art fallen, and
repent.*"

Man, being conscious of his own real position and of
the nature of this creation of Darkness
Maya, becomes possessed of absolute
power over it, and gradually withdraws all ˈthe developments of Ignorance. In this way, coming above the
control of this creation of Darkness *Maya*, he comprehends his own self as Indestructible and Ever-existing
Real Substance. So *Sat* the Existence of Self comes to
light.

How Existence
is realised.

All the necessities of the heart—viz., *Sat* Existence,
Chit Consciousness, and *Ananda* Bliss—
having been attained, Ignorance the
mother of evils becomes emaciated ; and
consequently all troubles of this material

How the main
object of the
heart is
attained.

world, which are the sources of all sorts of sufferings, cease for ever. Thus the ultimate aim of the heart is affected.

तदा सर्व्वंकामपूणोप रमार्थसिद्धिकात्

गुणानाम्प्रतिप्रसवे आत्मनः स्वरूप

प्रतिष्टा तदेब कैबल्यम् ॥ २२ ॥

22. In this state, all the necessities having been How Man gets attained and the ultimate aim effected, Salvation. the heart becomes perfectly purified and instead of reflecting the spiritual light receives the same ; and thus being consecrated or anointed by the Holy Spirit, becomes Christ the anointed, Saviour. Entering the kingdom of Spiritual Light, becomes the Son of God.

In this state man comprehends his Self as a fragment of the Universal Holy Spirit, and abandoning the vain idea of his separate existence unifies himself with the Eternal Spirit, i.e., becomes one and the same with God and Father. This unification of Self with God is *Kaivalya* which is the Ultimate Object of the created Being. Vide John XIV, 11.

"*Believe me that I am in the Father, and the Father in me.*"

————

CHAPTER III

साधन। THE PROCEDURE

तप: स्वाध्यायब्रह्मनिधानानि यज्ञ: ॥ १ ॥

मात्रास्पर्शेषु तितिज्ञा तप: । २ ॥

ब्रात्मतत्वापदेशश्चबसममननिनिधिध्यासंनमेव

खाध्याय: ॥ ३ ॥

प्रएवबशब्द एव पन्था ब्रह्मन: तस्मिन्

ब्रात्मसमर्पणं ब्रह्मनिधानम् ॥ ४ ॥

1-4 *Tapa* is religious mortification or Patience

Patience Faith and Holy works explained both in enjoyments and sufferings. *Shadhyaya* is *Shraban*, study, with *manan*, the attention and there by *Nidhidhyasan* ; forming of an idea of the true Faith about Self *i.e.*, what I am, whence I came, where shall I go, what I have come for, and such other matters concerning Self. *Brahmanidhan* is the Baptism or merging of self in the stream of the Holy Sound, *Pranava*, which

is the holy Work to attain salvation and the only way
by which man can repent to his Divinity˙ the Eternal
Father, whence he had fallen.   Vide Rev. II. 19.

"*I know thy works, and charity, and service, and faith, and
thy patience and thy works ; and the last to be more than the
first.*"

श्रद्धाबीर्य्यंस्मृतिमिमाध्यानुष्ठानात्

तस्याबिर्भाव: ॥ ५ ॥

स्वभावजप्रेमस्य बेगतीब्रताश्रद्धा ॥ ६ ॥

5-6, This Holy Sound *Pranova Sabda* appears
How the Holy
Sound appears
spontaneously through culture of *Sraddha* the energetic tendency of heart's
natural love, *Veerya* the moral courage,
Smiriti the true conception and *Samadhi* the true concentration.

This heart's natural love is the principal thing, to
The virtue of
Love
attain a holy life. When this love the
heavenly gift of nature appears in the
heart, it removes all exciting causes from
the system and cools it down to a perfectly normal
state, and envigorating the vital powers excretes all

foreign matters—the germs of diseases—from it by natural ways, perspiration, etc., and thereby makes man perfectly healthy, in body and mind, and enables him to understand the proper guidance of nature. When this love becomes developed in man, it makes him able to understand the real position of his own self as well as of other surrounding him. With the help of this developed love, man becomes fortunate in gettig the Godlike company of the divine personages and is saved for ever. Without this love man cannot live in the natural way, neither can he keep company of the fit person for his own welfare ; he becomes often excited by the foreign matters taken into his system through mistakes in understanding the guidance of nature, and in consequence he suffers in body and mind. He can never get any peace whatever and his life becomes a burden. Hence the culture of this love the heavenly gift is the principle thing for the attainment of holy salvation ; it is beyond doubt impossible for man to advance a step towards the same without it. Vide Rev. II. 2-4.

"I know thy works, and thy labour, and thy patience, and how thou canst not bear them which are evil : and thou hast tried them which say they are apostles, and are not, and hast found them liars.

"And hast borne, and hast patience, and for my name's sake hast laboured, and hast not fainted.

"Nevertheless I have some what against thee, because thou hast left thy first love."

शुद्धासेवित सद्गुरोः स्वभाबजोपदेशपालने

वीर्य्यलाभः ॥ ७ ॥

सब्बें एब गुरुवः सन्तापहारकः संशयछेदकः

शान्तिप्रदायकः

सत् तत्सङ्ग ब्रह्मवत्करनीयं, विपरीतमसत्

बिपबद्धञ्जनीयम् ॥ ८ ॥

7-8. As explained in the previous chapter, this creation is substantially nothing but a mere ideal play of Nature on the only Real Substance God the Eternal Father who is Guru—the Supreme—in this universe. All things of this creation are therefore no other substance than this Guru, the Supreme Father God Himself, perceived in plurality by the manifold aspects of the play of nature. Vide John X, 34, and Psalms LXXXII, 6.

"Jesus answered them, Is it not written in your law, I said, Ye are gods ?

"I have said, ye are gods ; and all of you are children of the most High."

Out of this creation, and object which relieves us
of our miseries and doubts, and administers peace to
us, however insignificant the same may be, whether
animate or inanimate, is entitled to our utmost respect,
Even it be an object of vilest contempt for others, it
should be accepted as Saviour *sat* and its company as
godlike which should always be kept. That which
produces the opposite results of destroying our peace,
throwing us into doubts, and creating our miseries,
should be considered *Asat* the bane of all good and
should be avoided as such. This idea led the Indian
sages to say—

"*Apshu deva manushyanam dibideva manishinam kash-
thaloshtrashu murkhanam juktashyatman devata.*"

Man to get salvation choose as their Saviour the
objects which they can comprehend according to their
own acquirements. Thus in general, people would
think that illness is a dire calamity, and as water, when
properly administered, tends to remove illness they may
choose for their Saviour or Divinity water itself. Philo-
sophers, being able to comprehend the internal electric
light which shines within them, find their heart's love
flow energetically towards the light that relieves them
of all exciting causes, cools down their systems to a
normal state, and envigorating their vital powers, makes

them perfectly healthy, both in body and in mind. They then accept this light as their Divinity or the Saviour. Ignorant people in their blind faith would accept a piece of wood or stone as their Saviour or Divinity in the external creation for which their heart's natural love will develop till by its energetic tendency it will relieve them of all exciting causes in their system and cool their system down to a normal state and invigorate their vital powers. The adepts, on the other hand, having full control over the whole material world, find their Divinity or Saviour in Self and not outside in the external world.

To keep company with one is not only to be with his person, but also to associate him with heart's love and to be one with him in principle. This has been very well expressed by Lord Bacon : "A crowd is not a Company, it is a mere gallery of faces." To keep company, therefore, with the god like object is to associate him with *sraddha*, i. e., heart's love intensified in the sense above explained, by keeping his appearances and attributes fully in mind, and by reflecting on the same and affectionately following his instructions lamblike. Vide John I. 29.

How to keep Company.

"*Behold the Lamb of God, which taketh away the sin of the world.*"

By so doing, when man becomes able to conceive the sublime status of his divine brothers, he may be fortunate in remaining in their company, and in

4

securing help from any one of them whom he may choose as his Spiritual Preceptor, *Sat-Guru* the Saviour.

Thus, to resume—*veerya* or moral courage can be obtained by the culture of *Sraddha*, *i.e.*, by devoting one's natural love to his preceptor, by being always in his company, and following with affection his holy instructions as they are freely and spontaneously given.

तद्वीर्य्यं यमनियमानुष्ठानात् द्रढ़भूमि: ॥ ९ ॥

अहिंसासत्यास्तेयव्रह्मचर्य्यापरिग्रहादय यम: ॥ १० ।

शौचसन्तोषसहृ रूपदेशपालनादय: नियम: ॥ ११ ॥

9-11. Firmness of moral courage can de attained by the culture of *yama*, the religious forbearances *i.e.*, abstention from cruelty, dishonesty, covetousness, unnatural living, and unnecessary possessions ; and by *niyama*, the religious observances, *i.e.*, purity in body and mind; cleaning the body externally and internally from all foreign matters which being fermented creates different sorts of diseases in the system, and clearing the mind from all prejudices and dogmas which make one narrow ; contentment in all circumstances ; and obedience to the holy precepts of the Divine personages.

To understand what natural living is, it will be necessary to distinguish it from what is

What is natural living ? unnatural. Living depends upon the selection of (1) Food, (2) Dwelling, and (3) Company. To live naturally, the lower animals can select these for themselves by the help of their instinct and the natural sentinels placed at the sensory entrances, viz, the organs of sight, smell, and taste. With men in general these organs, however, are so much perverted by unnatural living from very infancy that no reliance can be placed on their judgments. To understand, therefore, what our natural needs are, we ought to depend upon observation, experiment and reason.

First, to select our natural food, our observation should be directed to the formation of the organs which aid in digestion and nutrition, viz., the teeth and digestive canal ; to the natural tendency of the organs of sense which guide animals to their food ; and to the nourishment of the young.

What is Natural Food for man ?

By observation of the teeth we find that in carnivorous animals the incisors are little developed, but the canines are of striking lengths, smooth and pointed, to seize the prey ; the molars also are pointed ; these points, however, do not meet but fit closely side by side to separate the muscular fibres. In the herbivorous animals the incisors are strikingly developed, the canines are stunted though occasionally developed into weapons as in elephants, the molars are broad-topped and furnished with enamel on the sides only. In the frugivorous all the teeth are nearly of the same height, canines are little projected, conical, and blunt

Observation of teeth.

(not intended obviously for seizing prey but for exertion of strength). The molars are broad-topped and furnished at the top with enamel folds to prevent waste caused by their side motion, but not pointed to help in chewing flesh. In omnivorous animals like bears on the other hand, the incisors resemble those of the herbivorous, the canines are like those of the carnivorous and the molars are both pointed and broad topped to serve a twofold purpose.

Now if we observe the formation of the teeth in man we find that these do not resemble those of the carnivorous, neither do they resemble the teeth either of the herbivorous or of the omnivorous. They do resemble, exactly, those of the frugivorous animals : the reasonable inference, therefore, is that man is a frugivorous or fruit-eating animal.

By our observation of the digestive canal we find that the bowels of carnivorous animals are 3 to 5 times the length of their body, measuring from the mouth to the anus ; and their stomach is almost spherical. The bowels of the herbivorous are 20 to 28 times the length of their body and their stomach is more extended and of compound build. But the bowels of the frugivorous animals are 10 to 12 times the length of their body, and their stomach is somewhat broader than that of the carnivorous and has a continuation in the duodenum serving .the purpose of a second stomach. This is exactly the formation

Observation of the digestive canal.

we find in human beings, though Anatomy says that
the human bowels are 3 to 5 times the length of
their body—making a mistake by measuring the body
from the crown to the soles, instead of from mouth
to anus. Thus we can again draw our inference that
man is, in all probability, a frugivorous animal.

By observation of the natural tendency of the organs
Observation of the organs of sense. of sense, the guideposts to determine
what is nutritious and by which all
animals are directed to their food, we find that when
the carnivorous animal finds a prey, he becomes so
much delighted that his eyes begin to sparkle, and
he boldly seizes the prey and greedily laps the jetting
blood ; while, cn the contrary, the herbivorous animal
refuses even his natural food, leaving it untouched,
if it is sprinkled with a little blood. His senses of
smell and of sight lead him to select grass and other
herbs for his food, which he tastes most delightfully.
Similarly, with the frugivorous animal, we find that
their senses always direct them to fruits of the trees and
field. In men also, we find that their senses of smell,
etc. never lead them to slaughter any animal ; on the
contrary they can not bear even the sight of it.
Slaughter-houses are always recommended to be
removed far from the towns ; men often pass strict
ordinances forbidding the uncovered transportation of
flesh meats. Can flesh then be styled as the natural
food of man, when both his eyes and nose are so
much against it, unless his senses are deceived by

cooking with spices, salt, sugar, etc. ? On the other hand, how delightful do we find the fragrance of fruits, the very sight of which even makes the mouth water. It may also be noticed that various grains and roots possess an agreeable odour and taste, though faint, even when unprepared. Thus again we are led to infer from these observations that man was decidedly intended to be a frugivorous animal.

By the observation of the nourishment of the young, Observation of the nourishment of the young. we find that milk is undoubtedly the food of the new-born babe. Abundant milk is not supplied in the breasts of the mother, if she does not take fruits, grains, and vegetables as her natural food.

Hence from these observations the only conclusion Cause of Disease that can reasonably be drawn is that various grains, fruits, roots, and—for beverage—milk, and pure water openly exposed to air and sun are decidedly the best natural food for man. These being congenial to the system when taken according to the power of the digestive organs, well chewed and mixed with saliva, are always easily assimilated. Other foods are unnatural to men and being uncongenial to the system are necessarily foreign to it. When these foods get access to the stomach, they are not properly assimilated. Mixed with the blood, they accumulate in the excretory and other organs not properly adapted to them. When they cannot find their way out, they subside, in tissue crevices by the law of gravitation, and being fermented produce diseases, mental and physical ; and ultimately lead to premature death.

Experiment also proves that the non-irritant diet
Children's   natural to the vegetarian is, almost
Development. without exception, admirably suited to children's development both physical and mental. Their mind, understanding, will, the principal faculties, temper and general dispositon are also properly developed. We find that when extraordinary means such as excessive fasting, scourging, or monastic confinement are resorted to for the purpose of suppressing the sexual passions, these means seldom produce the desired effect. Experiment shows however that the man can easily overcome these passions, the arch-enemy of morality, by natural living on a non-irritant diet, above referred to ; thereby they get a calmness of mind which every psychologist knows is the most favourable to mental activity and to a clear understanding as well as to a judicial way of thinking.

Something more should be said here about the
      natural instinct of propagation, which
Sexual Desire. is, next to the instinct of self-preservation, the strongest in the animal body. Sexual desire like all other desires has a normal and an abnormal or diseased state ; the latter resulting only from the foreign matter accumulated by unnatural living as mentioned above. In the sexual desire every one has

a very accurate thermometer to indicate the condition of his health. This desire is forced from its normal state by irritation of nerves resulting from the pressure of foreign matter accumulated in the system, which is exerted on the sexual apparatus and is at first mani-fested by an increased sexual desire followed by the gradual decrease of potency. This sexual desire in its normal state makes man quite free from all disturbing lusts, and operates on the organism awaking a wish for appeasement only very infrequently. Here again experiment shows that this desire like all other desires is always normal in individuals who lead a natural life as mentioned.

The sexual organ (the junction of important nerve
The root of the tree of life. extremities, particularly of the sympathetic and the spinal nerves which are the principal nerves of the abdomen, which, through their connection with the brain, are capable of enlivening the whole system) is in a sense the root of the tree of life. Man well-instructed in the proper use of sex can keep his body and mind in proper health and can live a pleasant life throughout. The practical teachings of sexual health cannot be taught because, the public regards the subject as unclean and indecent. Thus blinded, mankind presumes to clothe nature in a veil because she seems to them impure, forgetting that she is always clean and that everything impure and improper lies in man's ideas, and not in nature herself. It is clear therefore that man, not

knowing the proper use of the sexual organ and being compelled to wrong practices by the nervous irritation resulting from unnatural living, suffers troublesome diseases in life and ultimately becomes a victim of premature death.

Secondly, about our dwelling place. We can easily understand, when we feel displeasure on entering our crowded rooms after breathing fresh air on a mountain top or in an expanse of field or garden, that the atmosphere of the town or any crowded place is quite an unnatural dwelling place. The fresh atmosphere of the mountain top or of the field or garden or of a dry place under trees covering a large plot of land and freely ventilated with fresh air is the proper dwelling place for man according to Nature.

Dwelling place of man.

And thirdly, as to the company we should keep. Here also, if we listen to the dictates of our conscience and consult our natural liking, we will at once find that we favour those persons whose magnetism affects us harmoniously, who cool our system, internally invigorate our vitality, develop our natural love, and thus relieve us of our miseries, and administer peace to us. This is to say, we should be in the company of the *Sat* or Saviour and should avoid that of the *Asat*, as described before. By keeping the company of *Sat* or Saviour, we are enabled to enjoy perfect health, physical and mental, and our life is prolonged ; if on the other hand we disobey the warning

Natural Company.

of Mother Nature, without listening to the dictates of
our pure conscience, and keep the company of whatever
has been designated as *Asat*, an opposite effect is produced and our health is impaired and our life shortened.

Thus natural living being indispensable to the practice
of *Yama* the ascetic forbearance as explained above, to make any attempt to practise *Yama* without living naturally is
altogether useless. Purity of mind and body being
equally indispensable to the practice of *Niyama*, the
ascetic observance as explained · above, every attempt
should be made to attain that purity.

Necessity of Natural living and purity.

ततः पाशक्षयः ॥ १२ ॥

घृणालज्जाभयशोकजुगुप्साजातिकुलमानानि

पाशाष्टकानि ॥ १३ ॥

तदा चित्तस्य महत्वम् वीरत्वम्वा ॥ १४ ॥

गार्ह स्थाश्रमापयोग्यासनप्राणायामप्रत्याहार —

साधनेषु योग्यता च ॥ १५ ॥

स्थिरसुखमासनम् ॥ १६ ॥

प्राणानां संयमः प्राणायामः ॥ १७ ॥

इन्द्रियाणामन्तर्मुखत्वम्प्रत्याहारः ॥ १८ ॥

13-18. Firmness of moral courage when attained
removes all the obstacles in the way of
salvation. These obstacles are of eight
sorts, viz., hatred, shame, fear, grief, con-
demnation, race distinction, pride of pedigree, and a

Meanness of human heart.

narrow sense of respectability, which are the meannesses of the human heart. By the removal of these obstacles,

How magnanimity appears. Beeratwam or Mahatwam (magnanimity of the heart) comes in and this makes man fit for the practice of Åsanam (remaining in steady and pleasant posture), Pranayamah (control over Prana, involuntary nerves), and Pratyaharah (changing the direction of organs, the voluntary nerves, inward.) These practices enable man to satisfy his heart by enjoying the objects of senses and are intended for Garhyasthashram (domestic) life.

Man can put the voluntary nerves into action whenever he likes and can give them rest when

Necessity of Pranayamah. fatigued. When all of these nerves require rest he sleeps naturally and by this sleep all these voluntary nerves, being refreshed, can work again with full vigour. His involuntary nerves, however, irrespective of his will, are working continuously of themselves since his birth, as he has no control over them he cannot interfere with their action in the least. When these nerves become fatigued they also want rest and naturally fall asleep. This sleep of the involuntary nerves is called Mahanidra, the great sleep or death. When this takes place, the circulation, respiration, etc., being stopped, the material body naturally begins to decay. After a while, when this great sleep Mahanidra is over, man awakes with all his desires, and finding his body unfit for further work leaves the same and goes somewhere else to create a new one for the accomplishment of his desires. In this way man binds himself to life and death and hence fails to get salvation.

But if man can control these involuntary nerves by the aforesaid *Pranayamah*, he can stop the natural decay of the material body and put the involuntary nerves to rest at times as is the case with his voluntary nerves. After this rest these involuntary nerves also become refreshed and work with a new life again. As, after sleep, when full rest has been taken by the voluntary nerves, no help is required to be awakened, so after death, also, when full rest has been taken by the involuntary nerves, no help is necessary to be in life again. If man can die, *i.e.*, put his entire nervous system to rest, controlling the natural decay of the body by the aforesaid *Pranayamah*, the nerves then being not much fatigued, life comes into play much sooner than after ordinary death and the whole system being refreshed begins to work with full vigour. Thus life and death come under control. In this manner man, saving his present body, from decay and from the terrible sufferings of death and requiring no further time for the necessary development of any other material body, can fulfil all the desires of his heart. Thus he is no more required to come into the world under the influence of darkness *Maya* and to suffer again a second death. Vide Rev. II 10, 11.

Control Over Death.

"*Be thou faithful unto death, and I will give thee a crown of life,*"

"He that overcometh shall not be hurt of the second death."

Man enjoys a thing when he so desires. At the. time of the enjoyment, however, if he directs his organs of sense through which he enjoys, towards the object of his desire, he can never be satisfied, and his desires increase in double force. On the contrary, if he can direct his organ of sense inward toward his self at that time, he can satisfy his heart immediately. So the practice of the aforesaid *Pratyaharah*, the changing of the direction of organs—the voluntary nerves—inward, is essentially necessary for the satisfaction of the worldly desires, by which man remains bound and cannot get salvation from the creation of Darkness, *Maya*.

Necessity of
Pratyaharah

Man cannot feel or even think properly when his mind is not in a pleasant state ; and the different parts of the human body are so harmoniously arranged that even if any minutest part of it be moved a little, the whole system becomes disturbed. So to comprehend a thing, *i.e.*, to feel a thing by the heart clearly, the practice of the aforesaid *Asanam*, the steady and pleasant posture, is extremely necessary.

Necessity of
Asanam.

चित्तप्रसादे सति सर्व्वभावोदय: स्मृति: ॥ १९ ॥

तदेवार्थमात्रनिर्भासं स्वरूपशून्यमिव समाधि: ॥ २० ॥

तत: संयम: तस्मात् व्रह्मप्रकाशक—

—प्रएवशब्दानुभव: ॥ २१ ॥

तस्मिन्नात्मनो योगो भक्तियोगस्तदा दिव्यत्वम् ॥ २२ ॥

19-22. Man, when expert in the above-mentioned practices, becomes able to conceive or feel all things of this creation by his heart. This true conception is called *Smriti*.

Smriti the conception.

Fixing attention firmly on any object thus conceived, when man becomes as much identified with the same as if he were devoid of his individual nature, he attains the state of *Samadhi* or true concentration.

Samadhi the concentration.

When man directs all his organs of sense towards their common centre the sensorium or *Sushumnadwarah* the door of the internal world, he perceives his God-sent Luminous body *Radha* or John, and hears the peculiar knocking Sound *Pranava Sabda* the word of God. Vide John I. 6, 7, 23.

Pranava Sabda, the Word of God.

"*There was a man sent from God, whose name was John.*"

"*The same came for a witness, to bear witness of the Light, that all men through him might believe.*"

"I am the voice of one crying in the wilderness."

Thus perceiving, man naturally believes in the existence of the true Spiritual Light and withdrawing his self from the outer world concentrates himself on the sensorium. This concentration of the self is called *Samyamah.*

Samyamah the concentration of self

By this *Samyamah* or concentration of self to the sensorium, man becomes baptized or absorbed in the holy stream of the Divine Sound. This baptism is called *Bhaktiyoga.* In this state man repents, *i. e.,* turning from this gross material creation of Darkness *Maya,* he creeps back towards his Divinity the Eternal Father whence he had fallen, and passing through the senssorium, the door, enters into an internal sphere *Bhuba-Loka.* This entrance into the internal world is the second birth to man. In this state man becomes *Debata,* a Divine Being.

Bhaktiyoga or Baptism the second birth of man

मूढविक्षिप्तक्षिप्तैकाग्रनिरुद्धाश्चित्तभेदास्ततः

जात्यन्तरपरिणामः ॥ २३ ॥

23. There are five states of the human, heart, viz., Dark, Propelled, Steady, Devoted, and Clean. By these different states of the heart man is classified, and his evolutionary status determined.

Five states of human heart

मूढ़चितस्य विपर्य्ययवृत्तिवशाद् जीवस्य शूद्रत्वम्,

तदा ब्रह्मएः कलामात्रेन्द्रियग्राह्यस्थूलविषयं

प्रकाशात् कलिः ॥ २४ ॥

24. In the dark state of the heart man misconceives,
The Dark Heart *i. e.,* he thinks that this gross material
portion of the creation is the only real
substance in existence and there is
nothing besides. This, however, is contary to the truth,
as has been explained before, and is nothing but the
Sudra or servant class effect of Ignorance *Abidya.* In this
state man is called *Sudra* or belonging
to the servant class ; because his natural
duty then is to serve the higher class people in order
to secure their company and thereby prepare his heart to
attain a higher stage. This state of man is called *Kali* ;
Kali.yuga the dark cycle and whenever in any solar system, man
generally remains in this state and is
ordinarily deprived of the power of
advancing beyond the same, the whole of that system
is said to be in *Kali-yuga* the dark cycle.

ब्रह्मएः प्रथमपादपूर्णे द्वितीयसूक्ष्मविषय

ज्ञानाप्राप्तसन्धिकाले चित्तस्य विक्षेपस्तदा

प्रमाएवृत्तिवशात् क्षतियत्वम् ॥ २५ ॥

ततः सद्गुरुलाभः भक्तियोगश्च

तदा लोकान्तिरगमनम् ॥ २६ ॥

25-26. When man becomes a little enlightened he
compares his experiences relating to the
The Propelled material creation gathered in his wakeful
Heart
state with his experiences in dream,
and, understanding the latter to be merely ideal, begins
to entertain doubts as to the substantial existence of the
former. His heart then becomes propelled to know
the real nature of the universe and, struggling to clear
Kshattriya the doubts, seeks for evidence to deter-
the Military mine what is truth. In this state man
classes.
is called *Kshattriya*, or one of the Military
classes ; and to struggle in the manner aforesaid becomes
his natural duty by whose performance he may get
an insight into the nature of creation, and attain the
Sandhisthal— real knowledge of it. This Kshattriya
the place state of man is called *Sandhisthal*, the
between
higher and place between higher and lower. In
lower
this state men, becoming anxious for
real knowledge, need help of one another ; hence
mutual love, the principal thing for getting salvation,
appears in the heart. By the energetic tendency of
this love man affectionately keeps company with those
who destroy troubles, clear doubts, and afford peace
to him ; and hence avoids, whatever produces the
contrary result ; he also studies scriptures of the divine
personages scientifically. In this way man becomes able to
appreciate what true Faith is, and understands the real
position of the divine personages when he may be for-
When man tunate in securing the godlike company of
gets sat guru,
the saviour some one of them who may kindly stand

5

to him as his spiritual preceptor *sat guru*, the saviour.
Following affectionately the holy precepts he learns to
concentrate his self, directing his organs of sense to
their common centre, sensorium. *Sushumnadwar* the
door of the internal sphere ; where he perceives the
luminous body John or *Radha*, and heard the holy
sound Amen *Aum* like a stream or river, and, being
absorbed or baptized in it, begins to repent (creep
back) towards his Divinity the Eternal Father through
the different *Lokas* the spheres of the creation.

भुर्भुव:खर्मेंहजनस्तप:सत्येति सप्त लोका: ॥ २७ ॥

27. In the way towards Divinity there are seven
spheres or stages of creation, designated as *Swargas*
or *Lokas* by the oriental sages, as described
in Chapter I, 16 ; viz., *Bhu Loka* the
sphere of gross matters ; *Bhuba Loka* the
sphere of fine matters or electric attributes ; *Swa Loka*
the sphere of magnetic poles and aura or electricities ;
Maha Loka the sphere of magnet the Atom ; *Jana-
Loka* the sphere of spiritual Reflection the son of God ;
Tapa Loka the sphere of the Holy Ghost the Universal Spirit ; and *Satya Loka* the sphere of God the
Eternal substance *Sat*. Of these seven places, the first
three, viz., *Bhu Loka, Bhuba Loka* and *Swa Loka*, comprise
the material creation the kingdom of Darkness *Maya*,
and the last three, viz., *Satya Loka, Tapa Loka* and
Jana Loka comprise the spiritual creation the kingdom
of Light. *Maha Loka* the sphere of Atom being in

The Seven
Lokas

the midst is said to be the door communicating between these two the material and spiritual creation, and is called *Dasamadwar* the tenth door, or *Brahmarondhra* the way to the Divinity by the Indian sages.

भुवर्लेके व्रह्मए: द्वितीयपादसूक्ष्मान्तजंगत्

प्रकाशात् द्वापर: जीवस्य द्विजत्वञ्च तदा

चित्तस्य क्षिप्तत्वात्तस्य व् त्ति विकलप: ॥ २८ ॥

28. When man being baptized begins to repent (creep back) towards the Eternal Father and, withdrawing his self from the gross material world the *Bhu Loka*, enters into the world of fine matter the *Bhuba Loka*, he is said to belong to the *Dwija* or twice-born class. In this state he comprehends his internal electricities the second fine material portion of the creation, and understands that the existence of the external is substantially nothing but mere coalescence or union of his fine internal objects of sense the negative attributes of electricities, with his five organs of sense the positive attributes, through his five organs of actions, the neutralizing attributes of the same, caused by the operation of his mind and conscience.

Dwija or
Twice-Born

This state of man is *Dwapara* ; and when this becomes the general state of the higher beings naturally in any solar system, the whole of that system is said to be in *Dwapara Yuga*. In this state, the heart becomes steady.

The Steady
Heart

If man continues in the baptized state, remaining
immersed in the holy stream, he gradually comes to
a pleasant state when his heart wholly abandons the
ideas of the external world and becomes devoted to
the internal one.

स्वर्गे चित्तस्यैकाग्रतया स्तस्य वृत्ति:स्मृति स्ततः

ब्रह्मएस्तृतीयपादजगत्कारए प्रकृति ज्ञानवशात्

तृ॒ता तदा विप्रत्त्वं जीवस्य ॥ २९ ॥

29. In this devoted state man, withdrawing his
self from *Bhuba Loka* the world of elec-
The Devoted
Heart tric attributes, comes to *Swa Loka* the
world of magnetic attributes, the electricities and poles ; he then becomes able to comprehend
Chitta, heart, the magnetic third portion of the creation.
This *Chitta*, as has been explained in chapter I, is
the spiritualized Atom *Abidya* or Ignorance a part of
Darkness *Maya*. Man, comprehending this *Chitta*,
becomes able to understand the whole of Darkness
Maya itself, of which *Chitta* is a part, as well as
the entire creation. Man is then said to belong to
the *Bipra* or nearly perfect class. This state of human
being is called *Treta* ; when this becomes the general
state of the higher being naturally in any solar system
the whole of that system is said to be in *Treta Yuga*.

महल्लोके चित्तस्य निरूद्धनतस्य वृत्तिनिद्रा

तत:सर्ब्बंविकाराभावे ब्रह्मवस्त्वात्मानुभवात्

ब्राह्मएत्वन्तदा ब्रह्मएस्तुरीयांशसत्पदार्थ-

प्रकाशात् सत्यम् ॥ ३० ॥

30. Man repenting (creeping back) further lifts up
his self to *Maha Loka* the region of
magnet ; then all the development of
Ignorance being withdrawn the heart
comes to a clean state, void of all external ideas. Then
man becomes able to comprehend the spiritual Light
Brahma, the Real Substance in the universe, which
is the last and everlasting spiritual portion in Creation.
In this stage man is called *Brahman* or spiritual
class. This state of the human being is called *Satya*
and when this becomes the general state of the higher
beings naturally in any solar system the whole of
that system is said to be in *Satya Yuga*.

The Clean Heart

तदपि सन्यासात् मायातीतजनलोकस्थे

मुक्त: सन्यासी तत: चैतन्यप्रक्टतितपलोके

आत्मानमर्पणात् सत्यलोकस्थे कैवल्यम् ॥ ३१-३२ ॥

31-32. In this way when the heart becomes perfectly
purified it does no more reflect but receives spiritual
·Light, the Son of God, and thus being consecrated or

anointed by the Spirit it becomes Christ the Saviour. This is the only way through which man, being again baptized or absorbed in Spirit, can rise above the creation of Darkness *Maya* and enter into *Jana Loka* the Kingdom of God, *i. e.*, the creation of Light. In this state man is called *Jiban Mukta Sannyasi*, like Lord Jesus of Nazarath. Vide John III. 5, and XIV. 6.

"*Verily, verily, I say unto thee, except a man be born of water and of the Spirit, he cannot enter into the kingdom of God.*"

"*Jesus saith unto him, I am the way, the truth, and the life : no man cometh unto the Father, but by me.*"

32. In this state man comprehends himself as nothing but a mere ephemeral idea resting on a fragment of the universal Holy Spirit of God, the Eternal Father, and understanding the real worship he sacrifices his self there at this Holy Spirit the altar of God, i.e., abandoning the vain idea of his separate existence he becomes dissolved or dead in the universal Holy Spirit; and thus reaches *Tapa Loka* the region of Holy Ghost.

In this manner, being one and the same with the universal Holy Spirit of God, man becomes unified with the Eternal Father Himself, and so comes to *Satya Loka*, in which he comprehends that all this creation is substantially nothing but a mere ideal play of his own Nature, and that nothing in the universe.

exists besides his own Self. This state of unification is called *Kaivalya*, the only Self. Vide Rev. XIV. 13 and John XVI. 28.

"*Blessed are the dead which die in the Lord from henceforth.*"

"*I came forth from the Father ; and am come into the world : again, I leave the world, and go to the Father.*"

CHAPTER IV

विभूति—THE REVELATION

सहजद्रव्यतपोमन्त्रभिः देहत्रयशुद्धिस्ततः सिद्धिः ॥ १ ॥

सद्गुरु कृपया तल्लभ्या ॥ २ ॥

सहजद्रव्येण स्थूलस्य तपसा सूक्ष्मस्य

मन्त्रेण कारणदेहचित्तस्य च शुद्धिः ॥ ३ ॥

1-3. Adeptship is attainable by the purification of the body in all respects. Purification of the material body can be effected by things generated along with it by Nature; that of the electric body by patience in all circumstances ; and that of the magnetic body (चित्त chitta) by the regulation of the breath which is called *mantra* (मनः त्रायते इति मन्त्रः) the purifier of the mind. The process of how purifications can be effected may be learnt at the feet of the divine personages who witness Light and bear testimony of the Christ consciousness.

साधनप्रभावेन प्रणवशब्दाविर्भाव-

स्तदेवमन्त्रचैतन्यः ॥ ४ ॥

देशभेदे तस्य भेदात् मन्त्रभेदः साधकेषु ॥ ५ ॥

(55)

4-5. By culture of regulation of the breath as directed by the spiritual preceptor *satguru*, the holy word *Pranava* or *Sabda* (प्रएब, शब्द) appears by itself or becomes audible. When this holy word *Pranava* or *Sabda* appears, mantra the breath becomes regulated and checks the decay of the material body.

This *Pranava* appears in different forms at the different stages of advancement according to the purification of the heart *chitta*.

शृद्धायुक्तस्य मद्गरुलाभस्तत: प्रवृत्ति-
न्दैव प्रवर्त्तकावस्था जीवस्य ॥ ६ ॥

6. It has already been explained what *Satguru* is and how to keep the company thereof. Man when endowed with the heavenly gift of pure love naturally becomes disposed to avoid the company of what is *asat* and to keep the company of what has been described as *sat*. By affectionately keeping the company of *sat* he may be fortunate enough to please one who may kindly stand to him as his *satguru* or spiritual preceptor. By keeping his godlike company there grows an inclination *Prabritti* in the disciple's heart to save himself from the creation of darkness *Maya*, and he becomes *prabartaka* an initiate in the practices of *yama* and *niyama*, the ascetic forbearance and observance necessary to obtain salvation.

यमनियमसाधनेन पशुत्वनाशस्ततः
वीरत्वमासनादिसाधने योग्यता च
तदैव साधकावस्था प्रवर्त्तकस्य ॥ ७ ॥

7. It may be remembered that by the culture of
yama and *niyama* the eight meannesses vanish from the
human heart and magnanimity comes in. It is at this
stage that man becomes fit for the practice of ascetic
posture, etc., the processes pointed out by his *satguru* to
attain salvation; when he continues to practise the
processes so pointed out to him he becomes a *sadhaka*
or disciple.

ततः भावोदयात् दिव्यत्वं तस्मिन्
समाहितेर्देववाणी प्रएवान् भवस्तदैव
सिद्धावस्था साधकस्य ॥ ८ ॥

8. On a reference to Chapter III it will be found
how a disciple, while passing through the different
stages, becomes able to conceive the different objects of
creation in his heart, and how he gradually advances to
the state of meditation, and ultimately by concentrating
his attention to the sensorium, he perceives the peculiar
sound *Pranava* or *Sabda* the holy word, when the heart

becomes divine, and the *Ego, Ahankara* or the Son of Man, becomes merged or baptised in the stream thereof and the disciple becomes *siddha*, an adept a Divine personage.

In the state of baptism *bhakti yoga, surat sabda yoga,* man repents and withdraws his self from the external world of gross matters the *bhuloka,* and enters into the internal one of fine matter the *bhubarloka,* where he perceives the manifestation of spirit the true light like seven stars in seven centres or conspicuous places which have been compared to seven golden candlesticks. These stars, being the manifestation of true light the spirit, are called Angels or *Rishis* which appear one after another in the right hand of the Son of Man, i.e., in his right way to the Divinity. The seven golden candlesticks are called the seven churches, *patals,* the seven conspicuous places in the body, known as brain the *sahasrara,* medulla oblongata the *ajnya chakra,* and five other centres, *viz.,* cervical *bisuddha,* dorsal *anahata,* lumbar *manipur,* sacral *swadhisthan,* and coccygeal *muladhar,* where the Spirit becomes manifested. Through these seven centres or churches, the *ego* or Son of Man passes towards the Divinity. *Vide Rev.* I. 12, 13, 16, 20 and II. I.

"*And being turned, I saw seven golden candlesticks, And in the midst of the seven candlesticks one like unto the son of man.........And he had in his right hand seven stars.*"

"*The mystery of the seven stars which Thou sawest in my right hand, and the seven golden candlesticks.*"

*The seven stars are the angels of the seven churches;
and the seven candlesticks which thou sawest are the
seven churches."*

*"These things saith he that holdeth the seven stars
in his right hand, who walketh in the midst of the
seven golden candlesticks."*

तत् संयमात् सप्तपातालदर्शनम्

ऋषिसप्तकस्य चाविर्भाविः ॥ ९ ॥

9. In this state of baptism *bhaktiyoga* or *surat sabda,*
yoga the Ego *surat* the son of Man, gradually passing
through the seven places mentioned above, acquires
the knowledge thereof; and when he thus completes
the journey through the whole of these regions he
understands the true nature of the universe. Withdrawing his self from *bhubarloka* the fine material
creation, he enters into *swarloka,* the source of all
matters, fine and gross. There he perceives the luminous
astral form around his heart Atom, the throne of
Spirit the Creator, provided with five electricities and
with two poles, Mind and Intelligence, of seven different
colours as in rainbows. In this sphere of electricities,
mind, and intelligence, the source of all objects of
senses and of organs for their enjoyment, man becomes
perfectly satisfied with being in possession of all objects
of his desires, and acquires a complete knowledge
thereof. Hence the astral form aforesaid with its
electricities and poles, the seven parts thereof, has

been described as a sealed casket of knowledge, a book with seven seals. Vide Rev. V. 1 and IV. 3.

"And I saw in the right hand of him that sat on the throne a book written within and on the backside sealed with seven seals."

"And there was a rainbow round about the throne."

नदा ज्ञानशक्तियोगक्रमात्
मप्नस्वर्गाधिकार स्नतश्चनुर्मणुनामाविर्भाव: ॥ १० ॥

10. Passing through this *swarloka*, the son of Man comes to *maharloka*, the place of magnet of which the ideas of manifestation, time, space, and particle (or atom) are the four component parts. As has been already mentioned in Chapter I, this *maharloka* represents *Abidya*, the Ignorance, which produces the idea of separate existence of self, and is the source of Ego the Son of Man. Thus man *manava* (मानव) being the offspring of Ignorance, and the Ignorance being represented by the four ideas aforesaid, these Ideas are called the four *Manus* (मनु+ष्ण = मानव) the origins or sources of man.

तन: भूतजयादणिमाद्यैश्वर्यंस्याविर्भाव: ॥ ११ ॥

11. The *maharloka* the place of magnet as explained before is the *Brahmarandhra* or *dasamdwara* the door

between two creations material and spiritual. When Ego the Son of Man comes to the door he comprehends the spiritual light and becomes baptised therein. And passing through this door he comes above the ideal creation of Darkness *Maya*, and, entering into the spiritual world, receives the true Light and becomes the Son of God. Thus man being the Son of God overcomes all bondage of darkness *Maya* and becomes possessed of all *aisharyyas*, the ascetic majesties. These *aisharyyas* are of eight sorts, *viz* :—

1. *Anima*, the power of making one's body or anything else as small as he likes even as an atom *anu*.

2. *Mahima*, the power of magnifying or making one's body or anything else *mahat* as large as he likes.

3. *Laghima*, the power of making ones body or anything else *laghu* as light as he likes.

4. *Garima*, the power of making ones body. or anything else *guru* as heavy as he likes.

5. *Prapti*, the power of *apti*, obtaining anything he likes.

6. *Basitwa*, the power of *basha, i.e.,* bringing anything under control.

7. *Prakamya*, the power of satisfying all desires *Kama* by irresistible will force.

8. *Ishitwa*, the power of becoming *isha* Lord over everything. Vide John XIV, 12.

"Verily, verily, I say unto you, He that believeth on me, the works that I do shall he do also ; and greater works than these shall he do ; because I go unto my Father."

तत: सृष्टिस्थितिप्रलयज्ञानात् सर्व्वनिवृत्ति: ।
तदा मायातिक्रान्ते आत्मानं परमात्मनि
दर्शनात् कैवल्यम् ॥ १२ ॥

12. Thus man being possessed of *aisharyyas* the ascetic majesties aforesaid fully comprehends the Eternal Spirit the Father, the only Real Substance, as Unit, the Perfect Whole, and his self as nothing but a mere idea resting on a fragment of the Spiritual Light thereof. Man, thus comprehending, abandons altogether the vain idea of the separate existence of his own self and becomes unified with him the eternal Spirit, God the Father. This unification with God is *Kaivalya* the ultimate object of this treatise. Vide Rev. III 21.

"To him that overcometh will I grant to sit with me in my throne, even as I also overcame, and am set down with my Father in his throne."

CONCLUSION

"Love rules the court, the camp, the grove,
The men below and saints above ;
For love is heaven and heaven is love."

The power of love has been beautifully described by
the poet in the stanza quoted above. It has been clearly
demonstrated in the foregoing pages that "Love is God,"
not merely as the noblest sentiment of a poet but as an
aphorism containing an eternal truth. To whatever
religious creed a man may belong and whatever may be
his position in society, if he properly cultivates this
ruling principle naturally implanted in his heart, he is
sure to be on the right path, to save himself from this
creation of Darkness *Maya*. It has been shown in the
foregoing pages how love may be cultivated, how by its
culture it attains development, and when developed
how, through this means only, man may find his spiritual
preceptor, through whose favour he again becomes
baptized in the holy stream, and sacrifices his self before
the altar of God, becoming unified with the Eternal
Father for ever and ever. This little volume is therefore
concluded with an earnest exhortation to the reader that
he may never forget that life is always unsafe and
unstable, like a drop of water on a lotus leaf, and that
the company of a Divine personage even for a moment
can save it, like Noahs ark in the flood. This thought

has been very poetically described by the Indian sage Shankaracharya in the following slokas—

"नलिनीदलगतजलमति तरलम्
तद्वज्जीवनमतिशयचपलम् ।
क्षएमिह सज्जनसङ्गतिरेका
भवति भवार्णवेतरणे नौका ॥"

THE END